# THIS IS
# THE KING!

## A Service For
## Palm/Passion Sunday

### BY CYNTHIA COWEN

## C.S.S. Publishing Co., Inc.
### Lima, Ohio

THIS IS THE KING!

9315 / ISBN 1-55673-568-5                          PRINTED IN U.S.A.

*This resource is dedicated to my congregational family at Christ the King, Escanaba, Michigan, for their affirmation and acceptance of my writing and participation in worship.*

# Table Of Contents

# Introduction

Sunday of the Passion, a service for Palm Sunday, announces the entry of the King of kings into Jerusalem and begins your congregation's Holy Week journey. The palms proclaim Jesus as Lord, as a special litany gives glory, laud and honor to the King. Jerusalem was churned up that week as Christ made his way toward Calvary. A children's message, "Churning Up The Waves," focuses in on Jesus, the Savior of our lives.

"This Is The King!", a dramatic three-part reading which replaces the sermon, declares that Jesus is King. In it Pontius Pilate journeys throughout the day being confronted with the prisoner, Jesus, who continually shows up in his court. This three-part dramatic reading offers a narrator guiding the action and making reflection while Jesus and Pilate add their words and thoughts. Costumes are optional. They make the event more realistic as the congregation is caught up watching the drama unfold.

The service continues to celebrate King Jesus with the sacraments of holy communion. "On that solemn night before his death, Jesus sat with those he loved. The cries of the crowd had died down. The Word had been proclaimed. Jesus had much to share with his followers. This would be the final opportunity. Tomorrow he would die. Jesus desired to leave with them the assurance of his presence whenever they gathered in his name *(opening of communion liturgy)*."

Truly, we remember our King as we break the bread and drink wine. We recall his love for this life and the passion it would call for in his death.

This resource enables worshipers to hail Jesus as King and to prepare to follow him to Calvary. Palms raised on high at the opening of the service declare Jesus' authority and announce his rule over humankind. Yet the soldiers who would scourge and mock him proclaimed, "Hail, King of the Jews!" in jest.

"As Christ was led from the presence of Pilate, he walked in submission to the Father's perfect will *(closing remarks)*." The service ends with a final reading from Mark 15:16-39 as the congregation hears of the love of God and his call to us to do likewise.

With this resource your congregation can declare "This is the King!" Pilate asked Jesus, "Are you the King of the Jews?" The soldiers offered him wine vinegar and said, "If you are the King of the Jews, save yourself." There was a written notice hung above him, which read, "This is the King of the Jews." This resource enables your congregation to declare the same.

# Lessons Of The Day

**First Lesson: Zechariah 9:9-10**

Rejoice greatly, O daughter
    Zion!
    Shout aloud, O daughter
    Jerusalem!
Lo, your king comes to you;
    triumphant and victorious is
        he,
humble and riding on a donkey,
    on a colt, the foal of a donkey.
He will cut off the chariot from
        Ephraim
    and the war horse from
        Jerusalem;
and the battle bow shall be cut
        off,
    and he shall command peace
    to the nations;

---

**Second Lesson: Philippians 2:5-11**

Let the same mind be in you that was in Christ Jesus,
    who, though he was in the form
        of God
      did not regard equality with
        God
      as something to be exploited,
    but emptied himself,
      taking the form of a slave,
      being born in human likeness.

And being found in human form,
   he humbled himself
   and became obedient to the
      point of death —
   even death on a cross.
Therefore God also highly
      exalted him
and gave him the name
   that is above every name,
so that at the name of Jesus
   every knee should bend,
   in heaven and on earth and
      under the earth,
and every tongue should confess
   that Jesus Christ is Lord,
   to the glory of God the Father.

---

**Gospel Mark 15:1-39**

As soon as it was morning, the chief priests held a consultation with the elders and scribes and the whole council. They bound Jesus, led him away, and handed him over to Pilate. Pilate asked him, "Are you the King of the Jews?" He answered him, "You say so." Then the chief priests accused him of many things. Pilate asked him again, "Have you no answer? See how many charges they bring against you." But Jesus made no further reply, so that Pilate was amazed.

Now at the festival he used to release a prisoner for them, anyone for whom they asked. Now a man called Barabbas was in prison with the rebels who had committed murder during the insurrection. So the crowd came and began to ask Pilate to do for them according to his custom. Then he answered them, "Do you want me to release for you the King of the Jews?" For he realized that it was out of jealousy that the chief priests had handed him over. But the chief priests stirred up the crowd to have him release Barabbas for them instead. Pilate spoke to them again, "Then what do you wish me to do with the man you call the King of the Jews?" They shouted back, "Crucify him!" Pilate asked him, "Why, what evil has he done?" But they shouted all the more, "Crucify him!" So Pilate, wishing to satisfy the crowd, released Barabbas for them; and after flogging Jesus, he handed him over to be crucified.

Then the soldiers led him into the courtyard of the palace (that is, the governor's headquarters); and they called together the whole cohort. And they clothed him in a purple cloak; and after twisting some thorns into a crown, they put it on him. And they began saluting him, "Hail, King of the Jews!" They struck his head with a reed, spat upon him, and knelt down in homage to him. After mocking him, they stripped him of the purple cloak and put his own clothes on him. Then they led him out to crucify him.

They compelled a passer-by, who was coming in from the country, to carry his cross; it was Simon of Cyrene, the father of Alexander and Rufus. Then they brought Jesus to the place called Golgotha (which means the place of a skull). And they offered him wine mixed with myrrh; but he did not take it. And they crucified him, and divided his clothes among them, casting lots to decide what each should take.

It was nine o'clock in the morning when they crucified him. The inscription of the charge against him read, "The King of the Jews." And with him they crucified two bandits, one on his right and one on his left. Those who passed by derided him, shaking their heads and saying, "Aha! You who would destroy the temple and build it in three days, save yourself, and come down from the cross!" In the same way the chief priests, along with the scribes, were also mocking him among themselves and saying, "He saved others; he cannot save himself. Let the Messiah, the King of Israel, come down from the cross now, so that we may see and believe." Those who were crucified with him also taunted him.

When it was noon, darkness came over the whole land until three in the afternoon. At three o'clock Jesus cried out with a loud voice, "Eloi, Eloi, lema sabachthani?" which means, "My God, my God, why have you forsaken me?" When some of the bystanders heard it, they said, "Listen, he is calling for Elijah." And someone ran, filled a sponge with sour wine, put it on a stick, and gave it to him to drink, saying, "Wait, let us see whether Elijah will come to take him down." Then Jesus gave a loud cry and breathed his last. And the curtain of the temple was torn in two, from top to bottom. Now when the centurion, who stood facing him, saw that in this way he breathed his last, he said, "Truly this man was God's Son!"

---

# *Order Of Service*

## Sunday Of The Passion
## Palm Sunday

### THE BLESSING OF THE PALMS

L: Let us rise and ask God's blessing on this celebration of the Sunday of our Lord's Passion.

Almighty God, we begin this Holy Week offering our time of worship unto you. We bring before you these palms, symbols of the praise and thanks we offer up to Jesus our Lord and Savior. Bless them as we wave them on high. May you be glorified in all we say and do.

C: **We praise you, O God and King. Hosanna!**

### THE PROCLAMATION OF THE PALMS

L: As Jesus approached Jerusalem and the cross, he stopped and received the praise of the people.

C: **Jesus, we hail you as our Lord and King.**

L: Christ told his disciples to go into the village. There they would find a colt tied to a post. They were to bring it to him. If anyone asked what they were doing, they were to say, "The Master needs it."

C: **Jesus, we confess our need for you.**

L: Returning to Jesus with the animal, the disciples piled their cloaks on it. Jesus then rode into the city.

13

C: Jesus, we confess our need to load our burdens and cares on you to carry.

L: The people threw garments and palms over the road shouting: "Hosanna! Blessed is the one who comes in the name of the Lord! Blessed is the coming kingdom of our ancestor David! Hosanna in the highest heaven!"

C: Jesus, we hail you as our Lord and King!

Processional Hymn: "All Glory, Laud and Honor"

L: Blessed is Jesus who comes in the name of the Lord!

C: Hosanna to God in the highest!

L: Let us pray: O Blessed King, we give you our thanks and devotion. Be exalted in our lives. Enable us to walk before you in humility. Increase in us obedience to follow where you lead. We spread our branches of praise in lives surrendered to your lordship.

C: Hosanna to God in the highest! Amen.


## THE PROCLAMATION OF THE WORD

**Anthem**

**First Lesson:** Zechariah 9:9-10

**Second Lesson:** Philippians 2:5-11

**Gospel Lesson:** Mark 15:1-15

**Children's Sermon**

**Hymn Of The Day:** "In The Hour Of Trial"

## PILATE'S DECLARATION

**A Dramatic Reading:** "This Is The King!"

**Special Music:** "Old Rugged Cross"

## CONFESSION OF FAITH

L: As Jesus was led out to die, we are reminded that his suffering and death opened for us healing and salvation. And so we confess our faith:

**The Nicene Creed:**
We believe in one God, the Father, the Almighty, Maker of heaven and earth, of all that is, seen and unseen.

We believe in one Lord, Jesus Christ, the only Son of God, eternally begotten of the Father, God from God, light from light, true God from true God, begotten, not made, of one being with the Father. Through him all things were made.

For us and our salvation He came down from heaven; by the power of the Holy Spirit he became incarnate from the Virgin Mary, and was made man.

For our sake he was crucified under Pontius Pilate; He suffered death and was buried. On the third day he rose again in accordance with the scriptures; he ascended into heaven and is seated at the right hand of the Father. He will come again in glory to judge the living and the dead, and his kingdom will have no end.

We believe in the Holy Spirit, the Lord, the giver of life, who proceeds from the Father and the Son. With the Father and the Son he is worshiped and glorified. He has spoken through the prophets. We believe in one holy catholic and apostolic church. We acknowledge one baptism for the forgiveness of sins. We look for the resurrection of the dead, and the life of the world to come. Amen.

**Announcements**

**Offering**

**Offering Response**

L: As Christ gathered his disciples around him on the night of his betrayal, he heard the cries of their hearts and of the world he came to save. Let us offer to God now the petitions of our hearts.

## THE PRAYERS OF THE CHURCH

L: Lord in our mercy,

C: **Hear our prayer.**

## WE CELEBRATE REMEMBERING OUR KING

L: On that solemn night before his death, Jesus sat with those he loved. The cries of the crowd had died down. The Word had been proclaimed. Jesus had much to share with his followers. This would be the final opportunity. Tomorrow he would die. Jesus desired to leave with them the assurance of his presence whenever they gathered in his name.

And so, the Lord Jesus took the bread, blessed and broke it. Giving it to them to eat, he said, "This is my body, given for you. Take and eat and remember me."

After the meal, he took the cup and blessed it. Giving it to them to drink, he said, "This is the cup of the new covenant of my blood. Drink and remember me."

When we eat this bread and drink this cup, we proclaim the death of our Lord Jesus.

C: **Christ has died. Christ is risen. Christ will come again.**

**The Lord's Prayer**

**Distribution Of Communion**

## PROCLAIMING THE KING WITH OUR LIVES

L: As we leave the Lord's Table, we remember we do not leave his presence, for Jesus is with us. May his spirit guide and direct us as we journey with him this week. We celebrate Christ with our lives lived out in faithfulness.

C: **Empowered by your body and blood, O Lord, we set forth to live for your glory. Amen.**

**Blessing:**

L: May the Lord bless you and keep you. May the Lord's face always shine upon you and be gracious to you. May the Lord bestow favor upon you and give you peace.

C: **Amen.**

L: As Christ was led from the presence of Pilate, he walked in submission to the Father's perfect will. Hear of his scourging for you that you might find healing. Hear of his death that you might find salvation. Hear of the love of God for you and his Son.

**Final Reading:** Mark 15:16-39

**Recessional Hymn:** "Ah, Holy Jesus"

# Churning Up The Waves

## Children's Sermon

How many of you like to swim? Do you like the water to be calm or rough? Often it is more fun when the waves are high. You can splash about rising over the whitecaps and plunging into the next series of turbulent water.

Waves are caused by currents in the water, currents which churn the water up. Jesus was like that on Palm Sunday — a strong current which would stir the waters of indifference in his people and cause ripples throughout history.

When Jesus entered Jerusalem, mounted on a donkey, he began the first wave. Children and adults stripped nearby trees of palm branches and began to wave them shouting, "Hosanna!" Hosanna means "save us." Now if we were at the beach and heard that cry, "save us," we would quickly look around for a lifeguard who might have a life preserver. We would trust that he would venture forth into the water to rescue the person in trouble. Today we shout "Hosanna," "Save us, Lord!" It is then that God throws us a life line. That life line is Jesus.

This day as we wave our palms and herald the Lord Jesus, remember that you are asking God to rescue you, to save you from sin. Jesus is that lifeguard who went out and dove into the waves of life and secured our salvation through his death on the cross. Grab hold tight of your salvation and let Christ pull you to safety.

Let us pray: Lord Jesus, thank you that when we are bouncing around in the troubled waters of life, we can call out to you to rescue us. We hail you as our Lord and King, our blessed Savior. We wave our praises like our palms and trust in your divine love to draw us from the drowning waters. Blessed are you, King Jesus. Amen.

# This Is The King

## Dramatic Reading
## Pilate's Declaration

**Narrator:** This Sunday of our Lord's Passion begins our Holy Week journey. Today we will listen to Pontius Pilate concerning Jesus as he declares, "This is the King!" The setting of our drama is Jerusalem. Dawn has just broken. We see Pilate slowly moving down the corridor of his palace.

**Pilate** *(Enters.):* "I hate mornings. The cock just crowed. It's too early to try a case — especially one involving a question of religion. I've had it with this group. Why couldn't I have been sent to rule over a less volatile nation?"

**Narrator:** Glancing down from the top of the marble staircase, Pilate carefully scrutinizes the crowd before him. Disgust fills his voice as he talks to himself.

**Pilate:** "I have to go to them. What a bunch of hypocrites trying to keep ceremonially clean! If their feet touch the stones of my gentile palace, they become unclean for their precious Passover celebration."

**Narrator:** Gathering up his robe, he made his way out to them.

**Pilate:** "Just look at that crowd. What a lowly lot. But wait — there — in the middle. That's the real source of discontent: those priests, elders, teachers. Hmmm . . . well, now. This is interesting. Looks like the whole governing body of Sanhedrin. I better watch myself with this cagey crew."

**Narrator:** As Pilate came to a stop before the seething mass of people, a man was thrust from their midst. *(Jesus enters.)*

He sized the man up with a soldier's experienced eyes. The prisoner looked as if he had had a rough night. Dressed in a wrinkled and soiled peasant's robe, the man stood before him with hands bound in front of him. None of the company around him looked very sympathetic. He stood alone. Most of the faces surrounding him were red with anger. Fists were raised. Snarls and curses rose from many. Motioning to a guard, Pilate spoke.

**Pilate** *(Aside.):* "I'd rather face the wolves of Germany than this mob. Get me a chair!"

**Narrator:** Sitting down, he raised his baton as a sign the trial could begin.

**Pilate:** "What accusation do you bring against this man?"

**Narrator:** Flippantly, the man's accusers replied that if he wasn't an evil-doer, he wouldn't be standing before the Roman official right now.

**Pilate** *(Aside.):* "Evil-doer? This guy doesn't appear to be such a vicious character. I've seen enough of those Jewish zealots to know. There's no fire in his eyes. No sneer of contempt for Roman authority on his face. Putting them down is a pleasure. Right?"

**Narrator:** His Roman body guard nodded agreement. Pilate looked at the prisoner again. This one who stood before him now seemed to be the only calm one in the bunch.

**Pilate** *(To the crowd.):* "Let's get on with this. I have a busy day ahead! In fact, this isn't any of my business. Take this man away and deal with him according to your own law."

**Narrator:** Howls of protest went up. "It's not lawful for us to put any man to death," they cried out.

**Pilate** *(Aside.):* "So that's what they want. His blood! They've come to use my rank and authority to gain their own ends. They'll use the system, and if I don't cooperate, those bigots will make sure Rome finds out. I need to get away from this mob so I can think straight. Bring the prisoner inside."

**Narrator:** Outside the crowds continued their murmuring. Inside the palace, there was silence. But inside Pilate's spirit, he felt a stirring he had not experienced before. Looking at the white robed figure before him, he tried to figure out why this man Jesus showed no fear. The question which now emerged from his lips startled even him.

**Pilate:** "Are you the King of the Jews?"

**Jesus:** "Do you say this on your own, or did others tell you this about me?"

**Narrator:** Pilate was startled to hear the authority and depth of the man's voice. He did not seem to be concerned about his circumstances. No pleading for mercy or protection. No fear of what might happen to him. He stood before Pilate as a captured king might have stood. With contempt in his voice, Pilate responded.

**Pilate:** "I'm not one of you Jews. Your own people have turned you over to me. Tell me what terrible thing you have done to get them so mad?"

**Narrator:** The silence caused Pilate to muse.

**Pilate:** "Look at this man. What has he done to enrage that angry mob? Messed with their religious system? Upset their financial apple carts? Those priests sit very comfortably taking in their temple taxes and offerings. They enjoy the prestige of their offices. Could it be that this man is threatening their little kingdoms?"

**Narrator:** The man's voice broke his train of thought.

**Jesus:** "My kingdom is not of this world. If it were just this world, my companions would have fought that I not be delivered to the Jews; but my kingdom is of another place."

**Pilate:** "Then you are a king?"

**Narrator:** He certainly talked like a king. Without anyone there to plead his case, this man Jesus stood with a definite majesty about him. Caesar had nothing to fear from such a king, though. Caesar was interested in the politics of this earth and the military advancement of his interests. This lone figure certainly was not plotting treason or spouting overthrow of the government.

**Jesus:** "You're right in saying I am a king. This is the reason I was born. For this promise I came into the world, to testify to the truth. All who are on the side of truth listen to me."

**Pilate:** *(Shrugs shoulders and talks to guard.)* "I tire of this examination. I've found out what I need to know. This prisoner is harmless." *(Pauses and turns to Jesus.)* "What is truth?"

**Narrator:** Going out to the crowd, Pilate delivered his verdict.

**Pilate:** "I find no fault with this man."

**Narrator:** His statement incensed the mob who cried, "He stirred up the people with his teachings all the way from Galilee to here."

**Pilate:** "I see. You've given me an out. Take this man to Herod then. I cannot try him. If what you say is true, he comes under Herod's jurisdiction. Take him away." *(Jesus leaves.)*

**Narrator:** Pilate returned to his quarters grateful to be rid of this Jesus person and his enemies. But why did he feel he was not done with this matter? Was this Jesus a king of a kingdom he had been searching for? The unfulfilled emptiness of the heart prompted him to consider this. Dismissing the thought, he lay down to rest. A few hours later his sleep was again interrupted by his guard. "Your lordship, the prisoner is back," he stated.

**Pilate:** "What? What? They're back? That blood thirsty mob is back? Darn that Herod! He's trying to get back at me. I tire of this. Let's get this over with."

**Narrator:** Angrily, he went out to the howling crowd. Weary of this matter, he sank into his chair again gloomily watching the events, which seemed to be out of his control, unfold.

**Pilate:** "What do I do with this king now?"

**Narrator:** Another guard entered and slipped him a note.

**Pilate:** "What's this? A note from my wife, Claudia. She never interrupts me. What's it say? 'Have nothing to do with this just man. I have suffered many things this day in a dream because of him.' "

**Narrator:** Pilate found himself unsettled by the note. Dreams often held warnings. Maybe he should heed his wife's advice. Leaning forward, he addressed the crowd again.

**Pilate:** "You've brought this man before me as one who is perverting the people. After examining him, I find no truth in the accusation. Herod evidently does not either, or he would have dealt with him. There is nothing that this man has done to deserve the penalty of death that you ask. Therefore, I'll punish him and release him."

**Narrator:** What an uproar occurred with that declaration. The mob did not want Jesus released. They began to chant, "Away with this man! If you're going to release anyone during this feast, give us the prisoner Barabbas!"

**Pilate** *(Throws up arms.):* "Great! They want a robber and murderer released. *(Shouts at the crowd.)* What harm has this Jesus done to you?"

**Narrator:** He had to shout to be heard, but the mob did not have ears to hear. Pilate watched as the priests moved among them, stirring them up.

**Pilate:** "What do you want me to do with this one you call the King of the Jews?"

**Narrator:** "Crucify him," began one, then another, until the whole mob was chanting in one accord. Pilate now looked out at the unruly mob with even more contempt than he had before. Curling his lips, he repeated for them their demand.

**Pilate:** "You want me to crucify your king?"

**Narrator:** "That will get them," he thought, and he was right. Enraged they shouted even louder, "We have no king but Caesar." They were setting him up, and he knew it. Holding up his baton, as a signal of authority, he proclaimed.

**Pilate:** "It is your custom to have a man released during this Passover festival. This man Jesus does not deserve death. But if it pleases you, I will let him go after my guards have scourged him."

**Narrator:** The angry crowd desired Jesus' death. "If you let this man go, you are no friend of Caesar's. Anyone who claims to be a king opposes Caesar."

**Pilate:** "There it is. They're threatening me, implying that they'll go directly to Caesar if this man isn't killed. Bring Jesus out." *(Jesus comes out again.)* "Here is your king."

**Narrator:** "Take him away. Crucify him," they shouted.

**Pilate:** "Do you really want me to crucify your king?"

**Narrator:** "We have no king but Caesar," they declared again. "We have a law, and according to that law he must die because he claimed to be the Son of God." A strange fear began to mount in Pilate. What was this turning into? He thought he was dealing with petty, religious jealousy, but now this Jesus was being labeled the Son of God?

**Pilate** *(Motions to Jesus.):* "Back inside." *(Pause.)* "Listen, Jesus, I want to know the truth. This whole thing is getting out of hand. Now, where do you come from?"

**Narrator:** Jesus looked straight at him and said nothing. Puzzled by the silence, Pilate again tried to get the prisoner to speak up for himself.

**Pilate:** "Why do you refuse to speak to me? Don't you know I have the power to free you or crucify you? I want to help you, but you seem destined to embrace a cross."

**Narrator:** Slowly, ever so slowly, and very clearly, Jesus spoke to his captor.

**Jesus:** "You have no power at all against me except that it has been given to you from above. Therefore, the one who handed me over to you is guilty of a greater sin."

**Narrator:** These words did not irritate Pilate. In fact, he found relief in them. The cries continued to rise as Pilate stood once more before the mass of angry faces. The group was in a frenzy of emotion. Pilate knew what he had to do. His eyes surveyed the madness before him. The paleness and weakness of the prisoner only made this trial even more a sham. He moved deliberately toward a basin of water which he had requested. He didn't have to make any more speeches. His actions would speak for his heart. Washing his hands before them, he deliberately took his time. They knew what he was doing. The tumult died down. Drying his hands with a towel, he stepped forward.

**Pilate:** "I am innocent of this man's blood."

**Narrator:** They understood and shouted back, "His blood be upon us and on our children!" Pilate had tried. His heart did not condemn him, but their words condemned their hearts.

**Pilate:** "Release Barabbas! Take the prisoner out and flog him. Then hang him on a cross. Make up a sign to put above his head. Make it so all can read: put it in Latin, Greek and Hebrew. It will say, 'Jesus of Nazareth, King of the Jews.' " *(Jesus leaves.)*

**Narrator:** Pilate made his voice heard that fateful day. He made a declaration with his words and actions that pointed to Jesus as King. When told to remove the sign, he refused.

**Pilate:** "What I have written, I believe, and it stands." *(Walks out.)*

**Narrator:** God calls to us at the beginning of this Holy Week to make a declaration with our lips and actions proclaiming the fact that Jesus is King. Go forth and do as Pilate did. Declare your king this Palm Sunday. Christ entered Jerusalem to the shouts and praise of the crowds and would enter Calvary's waiting arms to their shouts also. "Crucify him. Crucify the King!" Amen.

www.ingramcontent.com/pod-product-compliance
Lightning Source LLC
Chambersburg PA
CBHW071808020426

42331CB00008B/2438